Take a trip to
FRANCE

Jonathan Rutland

General Editor
Henry Pluckrose

Franklin Watts
London New York Sydney Toronto

Words about France

Alsace
Aubusson
Avignon

Bastille Day
Beaujolais
boules
Brittany
Burgundy

café
Carcassonne
centimes

Champagne
châteaux

écoles de ski

francs

grapes

Le Mistral
'left bank'

Mediterranean
Sea
Mont St. Michel

Paris
Parisians

'right bank'
River Seine

shutter
ski-ing
street markets

vineyards

wine

Franklin Watts Limited
8 Cork Street
London W1

SBN UK edition: 85166 860 7
SBN US edition: 0 531 00989 0
Library of Congress Catalog Card No:
80 52720

Printed in Great Britain by
Ebenezer Baylis & Son Ltd, Leicester.

Photographs are reproduced by kind
permission of Air France; The French
Government Tourist Office; Jonathan
Rutland; Barrie Smith.

Maps by Brian and Constance Dear.

France's most popular festival is
Bastille Day, which is held on 14
July. On 14 July 1789 the French
won their freedom from the King.
People buy flags to wave. There
are parades, carnivals and dancing
in the streets.

Sometimes school children go on outings to Paris. Paris is the capital of France. French school children work very hard at school. Even young children take heavy satchels of books home in the evening.

Many people visit Paris. They like
to go to the famous buildings, and
sit in one of the outdoor cafés.

Paris is cut in two by the River Seine. The largest part of the city is north of the river, and is called the 'right bank'.

The area to the south of the river is called the 'left bank'. Many artists live on the 'left bank'. There are also many outdoor stalls which sell books and pictures.

This picture shows some French
stamps and money. The units of
money are francs and centimes.
There are 100 centimes in a franc.

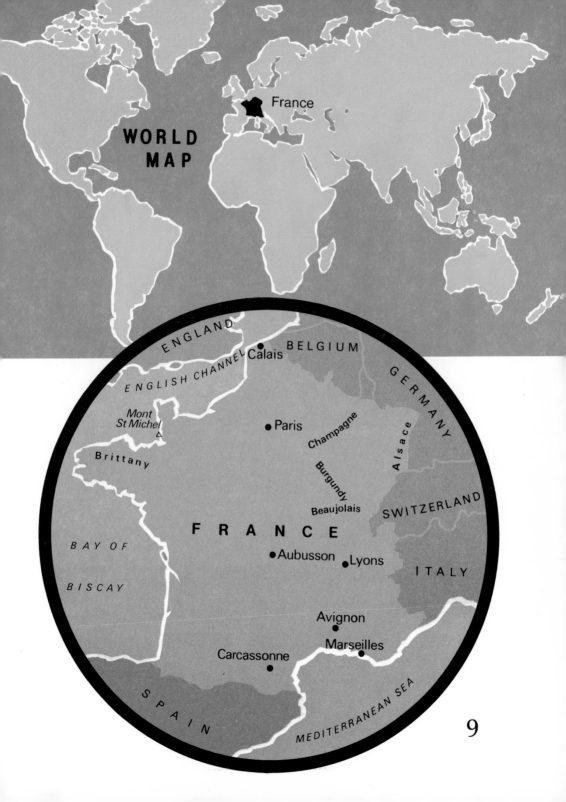

WORLD MAP

France

ENGLAND

ENGLISH CHANNEL

BELGIUM

GERMANY

Calais

Mont St Michel △

Paris

Champagne

Alsace

Brittany

Burgundy

Beaujolais

SWITZERLAND

FRANCE

BAY OF BISCAY

Aubusson

Lyons

ITALY

Avignon

Marseilles

Carcassonne

SPAIN

MEDITERRANEAN SEA

There are many very old towns
and buildings in France. Carcassonne
is an ancient fortress town. There
are thick walls around the outside
of the old town.

Avignon is best known for its bridge. It is the bridge in the song: *Sur le pont d'Avignon,* which means 'On the Bridge of Avignon'. The song tells how people used to dance on the bridge.

The middle of France is famous for its châteaux, or castles. But châteaux are more like palaces than castles. Many châteaux were built about 400 years ago.

The part of France near Germany is called Alsace. Alsace was once part of Germany and the people speak a mixture of French and German. Many of the towns and villages in Alsace have lovely old fairy-tale buildings.

The monastery of Mont St. Michel is in northern France. It is built on a tiny island. At high tide the island is completely cut off from the land by the sea.

In southern France are extinct (dead) volcanoes, mountain lakes and deep caves. Some caves have underground rivers and strangely-shaped rocks.

In France many people live in blocks of flats or apartments. The buildings have shutters in front of the windows. In warm weather some people dry their washing on the shutters.

16

Away from the big towns and cities, people live in houses or cottages. These homes are often built from local stone. They have shutters or blinds in the windows. There may also be a balcony.

The French often buy their fruit and vegetables in street markets. There may also be stalls of mobile shops selling fish or cheese. The food is produced locally. It is cheaper than in ordinary shops.

Wine is very popular and is cheap to buy. Even young children drink some wine with their meal. The main meal has many courses. The meat is often eaten separately from the vegetables.

The French railways are amongst the best in the world. This powerful locomotive pulls express trains like *Le Mistral*. *Le Mistral* travels from Paris to the South of France.

20

Large ports around the coast
handle big cargo ships. There are
also many small ports for fishing
boats.

Many parts of France have traditional costumes and customs from long ago. The costumes are kept for special festivals, fairs and parades, such as this festival day parade in Brittany.

Each region has its own special dances. There are many different kinds of folk-dancing groups all over France. These pictures show dancers and musicians from south-west France.

Boules is very popular with people of all ages. It is played on a patch of flat ground. Each player rolls his ball as near as possible to the main ball.

Ski-ing is very popular in winter. In some ski schools, or *écoles de ski*, children do school work in the morning and ski after lunch. In the highest mountains the snow never melts – even in summer.

The south of France is on the
Mediterranean Sea. There are long,
hot summers. In summer the beaches
are packed with visitors. They stay
in hotels, or in camping or
caravanning sites.

26

There are holiday resorts around France's other coasts, too. French children sometimes have special beach activities. They do exercises and play beach games.

French farmers are famous for their grapes. The grapes are made into wine. Many famous wines are named after the part of France where they are grown – like Burgundy, Beaujolais or Champagne. At harvest time people go to the vineyards to pick the grapes.

Later the juice is squeezed out of the grapes. Then it is stored in large wooden barrels. The wine may stay in the barrel for many years before it is bottled. Specially-trained people check the quality of the wine.

Some French people work in small workshops on all sorts of crafts. Aubusson is famous for its tapestries. Here you can see the bright wools being woven into Aubusson tapestry.

Other traditional craftsmen are the basket-maker and the potter. People can visit the pottery to watch the potter at work.

Boating holidays are popular both with French families and foreign visitors. By journeying through the countryside visitors can learn a little of the French way of life.